Kid's Box
New Generation

Caroline Nixon &
Michael Tomlinson

Workbook
with Digital Pack

American English

1

CAMBRIDGE

Acknowledgments

Many thanks to everyone at Cambridge University Press & Assessment for their dedication and hard work, and in particular to:

Liane Grainger and Lynn Townsend for supervising the whole project and guiding us calmly through the storms;

Alison Bewsher for her keen editorial eye, enthusiasm, and great suggestions;

Zara Hutchinson-Goncalves for her energy, enthusiasm, and helpful suggestions.

We would also like to thank all our students and colleagues, past, present, and future, at Star English academy in Murcia, especially Jim Kelly for his friendship and support throughout the years.

This is for Lydia and Silvia, my own "stars," with all my love. – CN

For Paloma, for her love, encouragement, and unwavering support. Thanks. MT

The authors and publishers acknowledge the following sources of copyright material and are grateful for the permissions granted. While every effort has been made, it has not always been possible to identify the sources of all the material used, or to trace all copyright holders. If any omissions are brought to our notice, we will be happy to include the appropriate acknowledgments on reprinting and in the next update to the digital edition, as applicable.

Key: R = Review, U = Unit

Photography

The following photos are sourced from Getty Images.

U1: romrodinka/iStock/Getty Images Plus; ViewStock; JGI/Jamie Grill; radnatt/RooM; Granger Wootz; Khosrork/iStock/Getty Images Plus; SchulteProductions/Photographer's Choice RF; **U2:** IlexImage/E+; skodonnell/iStock/Getty Images Plus; Coprid/iStock/Getty Images Plus; Anatoliy Sadovskiy/iStock/Getty Images Plus; deepblue4you/E+; Ko Hong-Wei/EyeEm; koosen/iStock/Getty Images Plus; Nichcha Sombutpanich/EyeEm; **U3:** broeb/iStock/Getty Images Plus; Yasser Chalid/Moment; pioneer111/iStock/Getty Images Plus; Nirut Sangkeaw/EyeEm; sweetym/E+; boitano/iStock/Getty Images Plus; malerapaso/E+; Puripat1981/iStock/Getty Images Plus; gldburger/iStock; underworld111/iStock/Getty Images Plus; John Lamb/The Image Bank; pekour/iStock/Getty Images Plus; John Smith/Corbis; **U4:** FlairImages/iStock/Getty Images Plus; Jose Luis Pelaez Inc/DigitalVision; Daniel Tardif/DigitalVision; fizkes/iStock/Getty Images Plus; SDI Productions/E+; Inti St Clair; twinsterphoto/iStock/Getty Images Plus; dszc/E+; 4x6/iStock/Getty Images Plus; Halfpoint/iStock/Getty Images Plus; kate_sept2004/E+; Juanmonino/iStock/Getty Images Plus; mdphoto16/E+; DjelicS/E+; Alejandra de la Fuente/Moment; Oliver Rossi/Stone; Image Source; Devi Sankar/EyeEm; Zach Krings/EyeEm; Philippe LEJEANVRE/Moment; Gary Mayes/Moment; Phillip Gatward/Cultura; fstop123/E+; HRAUN/E+; Silke Klewitz-Seemann; bymuratdeniz/iStock/Getty Images Plus; malerapaso/E+; AlexanderFord/E+; ajr_images/iStock/Getty Images Plus; John Rensten/The Image Bank; Morsa Images/DigitalVision; Kelvin Murray/Photodisc; Poike/iStock/Getty Images Plus; PT Images; Richard Newstead/Moment; RossiAgung/iStock/Getty Images Plus; Dimitri Otis/Stone; Images say more about me than words./Moment; Adastra/The Image Bank; Tokarsky/iStock/Getty Images Plus; Antonio M. Rosario/The Image Bank; buradaki/iStock/Getty Images Plus; Science Photo Library - SCIEPRO/Brand X Pictures; FatCamera/iStock/Getty Images Plus; Ariel Skelley/Photodisc; Mieke Dalle/Photographer's Choice/Getty Images Plus; R1-4: koosen/iStock/Getty Images Plus; malerapaso/E+; Puripat1981/iStock/Getty Images Plus; Devi Sankar/EyeEm; fstop123/E+; Kelvin Murray/Photodisc; Kinson C Photography/Moment Open; skodonnell/iStock/Getty Images Plus; Puripat1981/iStock/Getty Images Plus; JoKMedia/E+; Anatoliy Sadovskiy/iStock/Getty Images Plus; John Rensten/The Image bank; Sergiy1975/iStock/Getty Images Plus; hudiemm/E+; Creative Crop/DigitalVision; Philippe LEJEANVRE/Moment; malerapaso/Moment; loveguli/E+; Marianna Lishchenco/iStock/Getty Images Plus; triloks/E+; sweetym/E+; Coprid/iStock/Getty Images Plus; Alvaro Tejero/iStock/Getty Images Plus; Zach Krings/EyeEm; **U5:** GlobalP/iStock/Getty Images Plus; MediaProduction/E+; sserg_dibrova/iStock/Getty Images Plus; axelbueckert/iStock/Getty Images Plus; cynoclub/iStock/Getty Images Plus; GlobalP/iStock/Getty Images Plus; raw/iStock/Getty Images Plus; Andregric/iStock/Getty Images Plus; Dougal Waters/DigitalVision; Parkpoom Doungkaew/EyeEm; Elles Rijsdijk/EyeEm; Algefoto/iStock/Getty Images Plus; Adrian Coleman/E+; nigelb10/iStock/Getty Images Plus; Engdao Wichitpunya/EyeEm; Péter Hegedűs/500px Prime; Georgette Douwma/Stockbyte;

U6: strike0/iStock/Getty Images Plus; Alastair Pollock Photography/Moment; Szilvia Pap-Kutasi/500px; Roy JAMES Shakespeare/Photodisc; Westend61; bubaone/DigitalVision Vectors; Christopher Hopefitch/DigitalVision; Yellow Dog Productions/The Image Bank; simonlong/Moment; Nils Jacobi/iStock/Getty Images Plus; **U7:** Olga Kurbatova/iStock/Getty Images Plus; **U8:** simonlong/Stone; goinyk/iStock/Getty Images Plus; Matteo Colombo/Moment; Ethel Peisker Lacerda/EyeEm; elmvilla/iStock/Getty Images Plus; Patrice Hauser/The Image Bank/Getty Images Plus; David Rowland/The Image Bank/Getty Images Plus; Mark Hamblin/Oxford Scientific/Getty Images Plus; QuimGranell/Moment/Getty Images Plus; Lian van den Heever/Gallo Images/Getty Images Plus; kuritafsheen/RooM; Rafael Ben-Ari/The Image Bank/Getty Images Plus; fstop123/E+; Imgorthand/E+; Dean Mitchell/E+; Jose Luis Pelaez Inc/DigitalVision; Artyom Kozhemyakin/iStock/Getty Images Plus; R5-8: Georgette Douwma/Stone; ToscaWhi/iStock/Getty Images Plus; Patricia Doyle/Corbis Documentary; Sergey Ryumin/Moment; Ignacio Palacios/Stone; Darren Robb/The Image Bank; Ulli Bonnekamp/Photodisc; **U9:** StockPlanets/E+; Stockbyte; Santiago Urquijo/Moment; maccj/iStock/Getty Images Plus; Kris Timken; HRAUN/E+; Fabio Alcini/500Px Plus; simonlong/Moment; Rafa Fernández/EyeEm; ilbusca/iStock/Getty Images Plus; Tim Hawley/Photographer's Choice/Getty Images Plus; Fajrul Islam/Moment; monkeybusinessimages/iStock/Getty Images Plus; Tsuneo Yamashita/Taxi Japan/Getty Images Plus; Zero Creatives/Cultura; Stas Zakshevskiy/EyeEm; David Madison/Stone; master1305/iStock/Getty Images Plus; Gearstd/iStock/Getty Images Plus; Photodisc; Nalinratana Phiyanalinmat/EyeEm; Drazen Stader/EyeEm; Andriy Onufriyenko/Moment; Samus Henderson/EyeEm; Johner Images; SasinT Gallery/Moment; **U10:** Adamo Di Loreto/iStock/Getty Images Plus; anhoog/iStock/Getty Images Plus; phive2015/iStock/Getty Images Plus; alxpin/E+; Henglein And Steets/Photolibrary; Carl & Ann Purcell/The Image Bank Unreleased; Andrius Aleksandravicius/EyeEm; Henglein And Steets/Photolibrary; Tryaging/iStock; prospective56/iStock/Getty Images Plus; avid_creative/E+; Zia Soleil/Stone; kali9/E+; Katja Zimmermann/The Image Bank; FatCamera/E+; **U11:** Letizia Le Fur/ONOKY; Jeff Greenough; Wealan Pollard/OJO Images; vgajic/iStock/Getty Images Plus; JGI/Jamie Grill; Patricia Abecina/EyeEm; Gearstd/iStock/Getty Images Plus; 3dgoksu/E+; Eduard Lysenko/iStock/Getty Images Plus; C Squared Studios/Photodisc; kemalbas/iStock/Getty Images Plus; **U12:** MichaelJay/iStock/Getty Images Plus; Wealthylady/iStock/Getty Images Plus; vfoto/iStock/Getty Images Plus; Westend61; Ljupco/iStock/Getty Images Plus; unpict/iStock/Getty Images Plus; Nattawut Lakjit/EyeEm; tunart/E+; Voren1/iStock/Getty Images Plus; Stockbyte; popovaphoto/iStock/Getty Images Plus; robertsre/iStock/Getty Images Plus; bergamont/iStock/Getty Images Plus; Michael Burrell/iStock/Getty Images Plus; BWFolsom/iStock/Getty Images Plus; ThinkDeep/E+; carlosalvarez/iStock/Getty Images Plus; arkstart/iStock/Getty Images Plus; Thor Hakonsen/Moment Open; Martin Harvey/DigitalVision; GlobalP/iStock/Getty Images Plus; vusta/E+; gerenme/E+; Dmytro Synelnychenko/iStock/Getty Images Plus; Renaud Philippe/EyeEm; wilatlak villette/Moment; Nenov/Moment; digitalgenetics/iStock/Getty Images Plus; Wong Sze Fei/EyeEm; Antagain/E+; eli_asenova/iStock/Getty Images Plus; DNY59/E+; CasarsaGuru/iStock/Getty Images Plus; xavierarnau/E+; Zuzana Janekova/EyeEm; Jill Giardino; JanuarySkyePhotography/Moment; LindaYolanda/E+; Ross Whitaker/The Image Bank; Kelvin Murray/Phtodisc; damircudic/E+.

The following photos are sourced from other libraries.

U2: Gino Santa Maria/Shutterstock; **U4:** Halfpoint/Shutterstock. Commissioned photography by Trevor Clifford Photography.

Illustrations

Beth Hughes (The Bright Agency); Clara Soriano (The Bright Agency); Dan Crisp (The Bright Agency); Jen Naalchigar (The Bright Agency); Gaby Zermeno (Direct artist); Jake McDonald (The Bright Agency); Matthew Scott (The Bright Agency); Pronk Media Inc.
Cover illustration by Pronk Media Inc

Audio

Audio managed by Hyphen Publishing, produced by New York Audio Productions and John Marshall Media.
Songs composed by Robert Lee.

Typeset

Blooberry Design

Contents

1 Hi!

1 Look and match.

2 🎧 2 Listen and circle the ✓ or ✗.

1. ✓ ✗
2. ✓ ✗
3. ✓ ✗
4. ✓ ✗

Vocabulary: character names   ▸ Do the online activities on **Practice Extra** as you complete this unit.

Look, match, and say.

 Connect the dots.

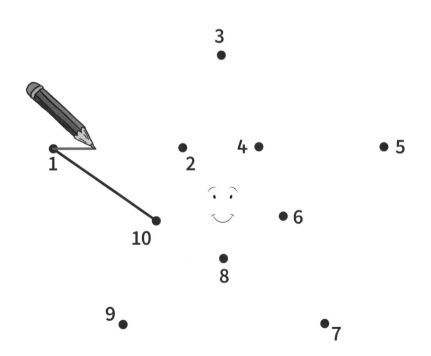

1 🎧 3 Listen and write the number.

 6

2 Draw and write.

Me!

I'm ___ Paula ___ .
I'm ___ seven ___ .

Me!

I'm _____ .
I'm _____ .

Starters Listening

1 🎧 4 🐵 **Listen and color.**

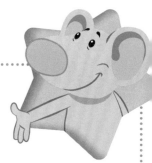

 Look, circle, and color.

r

2 **Write and draw.**

_ed _ainbow

My picture dictionary

1 **Find and stick.**

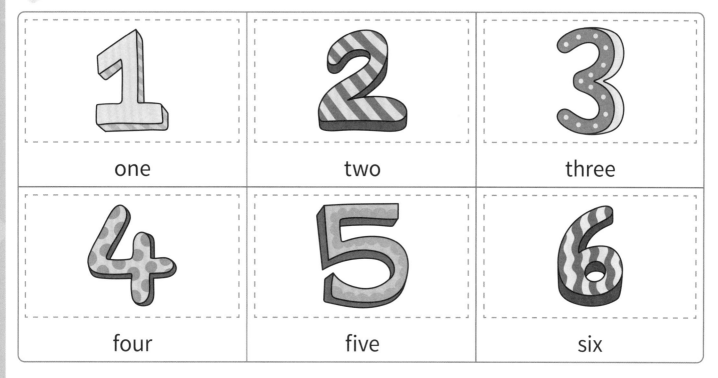

one	two	three
four	five	six

My star card

2 **Say the words. Color the stars.**

2 My school

1 🎧 5 **Listen and color.**

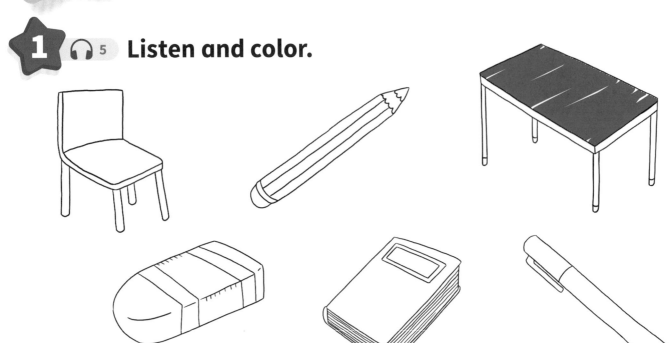

2 **Draw your table. Say.**

> The table is blue. The book is red.

Me!

Me!

📱 Do the online activities on **Practice Extra** as you complete this unit.

Draw three pictures.

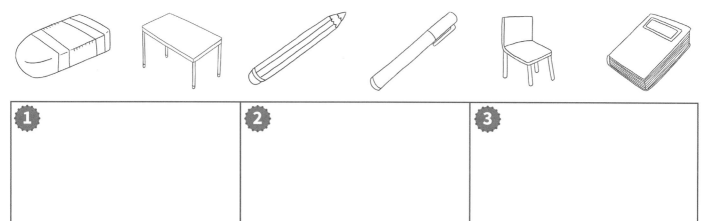

1	2	3

Tell your friend.
Draw your friend's pictures.

Number one is a chair.

1	2	3

2 **Count and write the number. Say.**

Tables. Four!

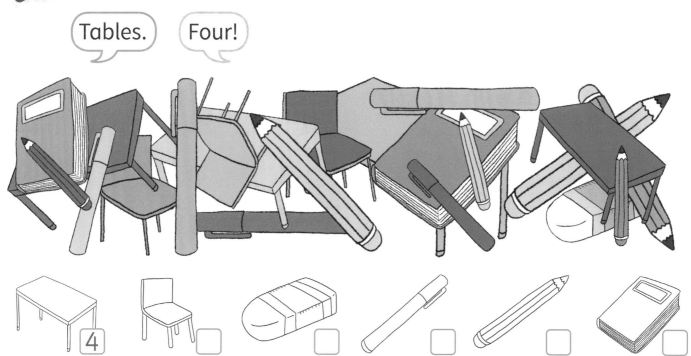

 🎧 6 **Listen and write the number.**

2 **Follow the lines and say.**

Language: question words *How old is he/she? He's/She's (nine).*

Starters Reading and Writing

1 **Look and read. Put a ✓ or an ✗ in the box .**

Example

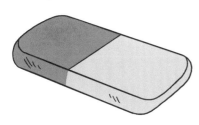

This is a pencil. ✗

Questions

1

This is a book. ☐

2

This is a table. ☐

3

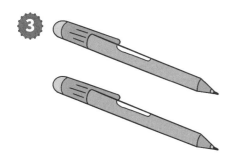

These are erasers. ☐

4

This is a bag. ☐

Monty's sounds and spelling

 1 **Read and match.**

book   bag

pencil   pen

 2 **Look and draw.**

p

b

My picture dictionary

1 Find and stick.

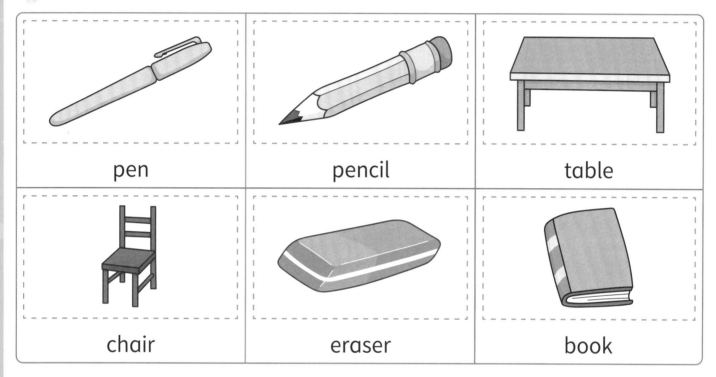

pen	pencil	table
chair	eraser	book

My star card

2 Say the words. Color the stars.

Marie's Art

What happens when you mix colors?

1  7 **Listen and color. Say.**

1 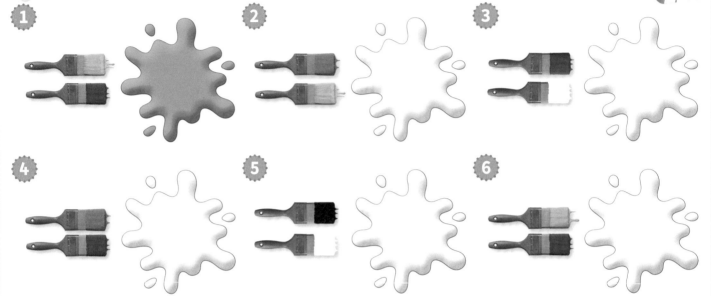 2 3

4 5 6

2 **Look and write. Circle the pictures of primary colors.**

 red   blue   yellow

purple

pink

orange

green

3 Now you! **Play and say.**   This is a purple pencil.

16   Art: mix colors | critical thinking

Trevor's values

Make friends

 1 **Draw and color two friends.**
Ask, answer, and write.

What's your name? How old are you?

I'm ___Sam___.
I'm ___seven___.

I'm _____.
I'm _____.

I'm _____.
I'm _____.

3 Favorite toys

1 🎧 8 Listen and circle the ✓ or ✗.

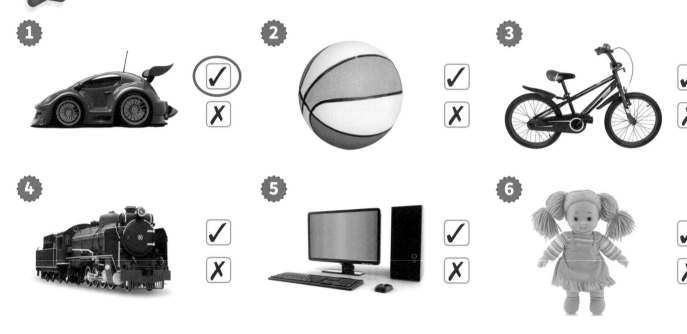

1 ✓ ✗

2 ✓ ✗

3 ✓ ✗

4 ✓ ✗

5 ✓ ✗

6 ✓ ✗

2 Look and match. Say.

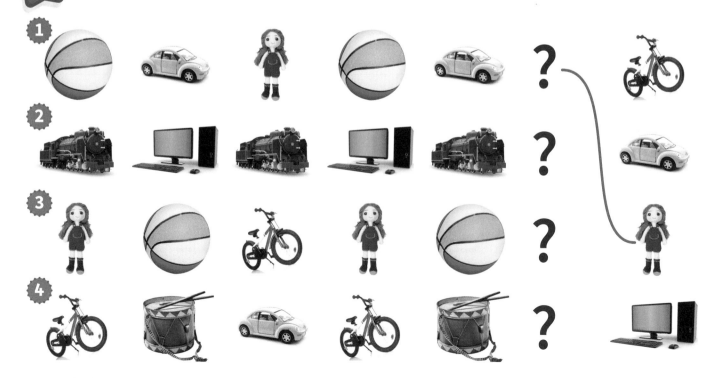

1

2

3

4

⬚ Do the online activities on **Practice Extra** as you complete this unit.

1 🎧 9 Listen and draw colored lines.

2 Color the toys.

Now ask and answer. Color your friend's toys.

What color's your ball?　It's green.

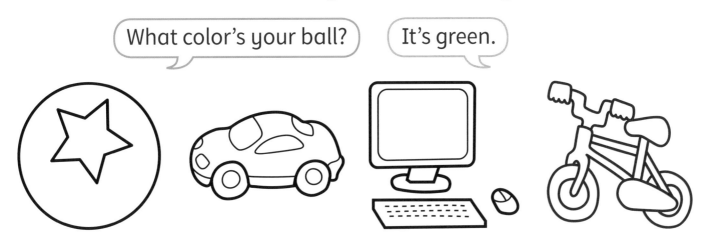

 **1** 🎧 10 **Listen and write the number.**

☐ ☐ ☐

☐ ☐ 1

2 **Find and circle the differences.**

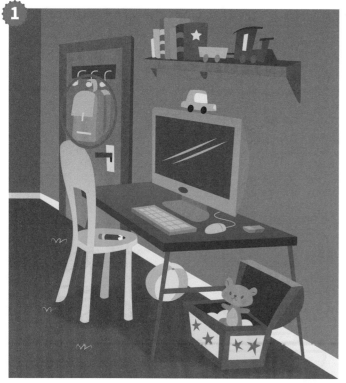

Language: prepositions of place *It's in / on / under / next to the (train).*

Starters Listening

1 🎧 11 🐵 **Listen and draw lines.**

Matt   Alice   Hugo

Eva   Mark   Mary

monty's sounds and spelling

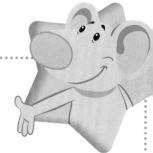

1 🎧 12 **Listen and circle "t" or "d."**

1 ⓣ d   2 t d   3 t d   4 t d

5 t d   6 t d   7 t d   8 t d

2 **Look and write "t" or "d."**

__oll

__rum

__able

__rain

__wo __eddies

My picture dictionary

1 **Find and stick.**

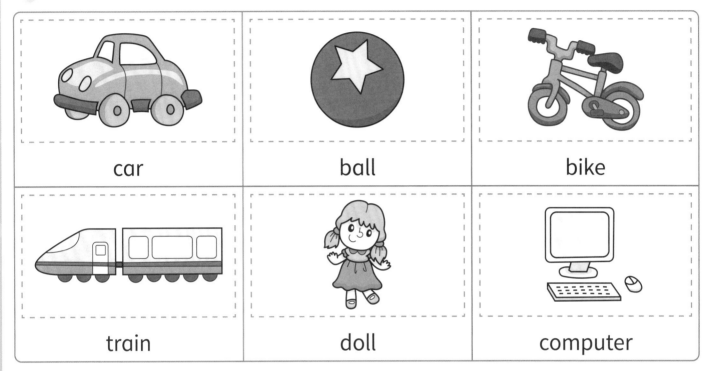

| car | ball | bike |
| train | doll | computer |

My star card

2 **Say the words. Color the stars.**

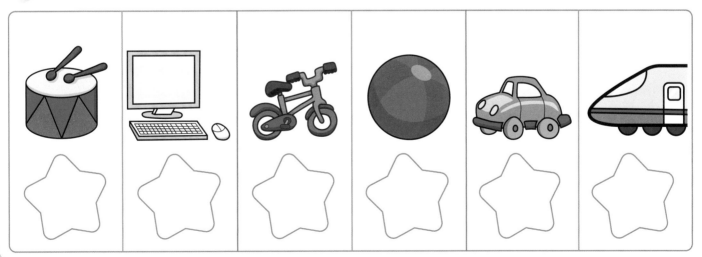

4 My family

1 Look and write the number. Say.

Number 1!

Sally. His sister.

1 Sally   2 Mr. Star   3 Grandpa Star
4 Mrs. Star   5 Suzy   6 Grandma Star

 1

2 🎧 13 Listen and color.

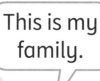

This is my family.

Vocabulary: family

▶ Do the online activities on Practice Extra as you complete this unit.

1 🎧 14 Listen and draw colored lines.

2 Draw your family. Say.

He's my brother.

Me!

1 🎧 15 **Listen and color the stars.**

This is my family.

2 **Look and circle. Say and guess.**

Happy. Happy. Sad. Happy.

Number 1.

Language: adjectives *She's (young).*

Starters Reading and Writing

1  Look and complete the words.

Example

b e a u t i f u l

f t b a i
u e l u

Questions

 1

o   d   l

 2

d   s   a

 3

u y
l   g

 4

p   h y
p   a

 5

u y g
n   o

Monty's sounds and spelling

1 🎧 16 **Listen and circle the "a" in the words.**

1 c@t

2 s a d

3 b a g

4 h a p p y

5 f a m i l y

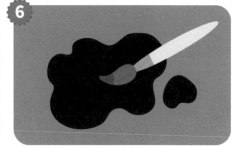

6 b l a c k

2 **Look and match.**

hat

dad

happy

cat

black

1

2

3

4

5

My picture dictionary

1 **Find and stick.**

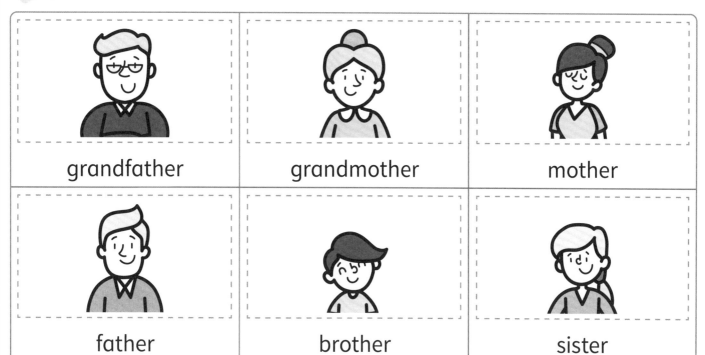

grandfather	grandmother	mother
father	brother	sister

My star card

2 **Say the words. Color the stars.**

Marie's science

Which planets are near Earth?

 Look, read, and check (✓).

This is the planet where we live.

Earth ✓
Jupiter ☐

This planet is called "the red planet."

Venus ☐
Mars ☐

This planet is very big.

Mercury ☐
Jupiter ☐

This planet is next to the sun.

Mercury ☐
Earth ☐

 Look and write.   the sun   Earth   Jupiter

_____   _____   _____

 Now you! **Play and say.**

I'm a red planet.

You're Mars!

Trevor's values

Be kind

 Look, read, and write the number.

1

Here you are.

OK!

2

Let's clean up!

That's OK.

3

I'm sorry.

Thank you!

1

Language: *Here you are. Thank you. I'm sorry. That's OK. Let's clean up!* | 🛡 emotional development

1 🎧 17 Listen and connect the dots.

What's this?

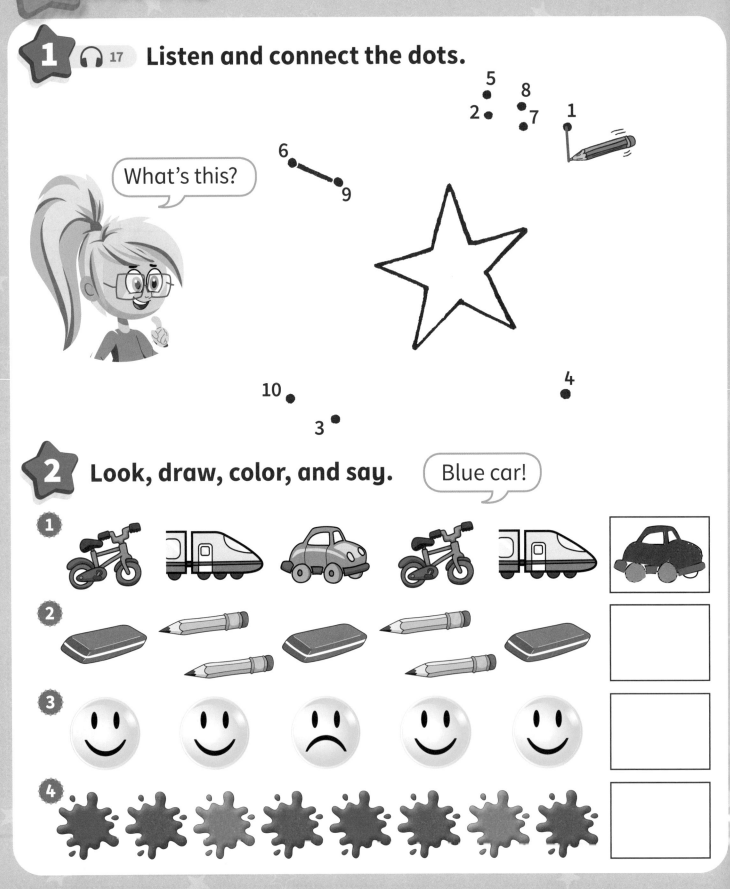

2 Look, draw, color, and say.

Blue car!

3 Say, look, and answer.

Purple, one. He's young! Green, three. It's a car!

1 **2** **3** **4** **5**

5 Our pets

1 🎧 18 Listen and circle the ✓ or ✗.

1  ☑ ✓ ☐ ✗

2  ☐ ✓ ☐ ✗

3  ☐ ✓ ☐ ✗

4  ☐ ✓ ☐ ✗

5  ☐ ✓ ☐ ✗

6  ☐ ✓ ☐ ✗

2 Look and write.

a bird   a cat   a dog   a fish   a horse   ~~a mouse~~

1
a mouse

2

3

4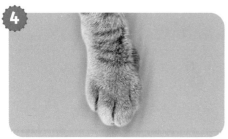

5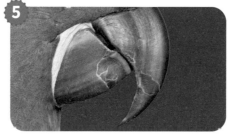

6

1 Color the pets.

Now ask and answer. Color your friend's pets.

What color is the fish?

It's blue.

2 Read and write the answer.

birds   ~~fish~~   mice   cats   horses

1 What are they?
They're _____fish_____ .

2 What are they?
They're _____ .

3 What are they?
They're _____ .

4 What are they?
They're _____ .

5 What are they?
They're _____ .

Look, read, and circle.

1

short /(long)

2

clean / dirty

3

small / big

4

short / long

5

big / small

6

clean / dirty

2 🎧 19 **Listen and follow.**

Language: adjectives *They're (clean).*

Starters Reading and Writing

1 **Look and read. Put a ✓ or an ✗ in the box.**

Example

This is a horse.   ✓

Questions

These are birds.   ☐

This is a mouse.   ☐

This is a cat.   ☐

This is a fish.   ☐

monty's sounds and spelling

1 Draw lines to make two words.

r ⌒ e
p   e   d   t

2 Look and write.

My r _ _ _ p _ _ _ .

3 🎧 20 Listen and write "a" or "e."

p e t s   b _ g   c _ t   p _ n

t _ n   s _ d   S _ lly   h _ ppy

My picture dictionary

1 **Find and stick.**

? ? ? ?	? ? ? ?	? ? ? ?
dog	bird	cat
? ? ? ?	? ? ? ?	? ? ? ?
fish	mouse	horse

My star card

2 **Say the words. Color the stars.**

6 My face

1 🎧 21 **Listen and draw colored lines.**

2 **Circle the different word.**

1 (table)	horse	mouse	bird
2 bike	nose	train	doll
3 eyes	ears	teeth	ball
4 book	pen	car	pencil
5 fish	horse	cat	head
6 dog	four	ten	seven

Vocabulary: the face   📲 Do the online activities on **Practice Extra** as you complete this unit.

 **1** 🎧 22 **Listen and write the number.**

 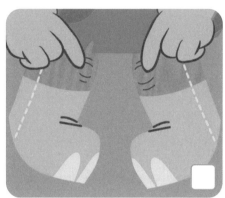 

 2 **Look and write.**

| e | a | r | s | | e | y | e | s | | n | o | s | e | | m | o | u | t | h |

| t | e | e | t | h |

| h | a | i | r |

| e | a | r | s |

 **1** 🎧 23 **Listen and draw. Listen and color.**

2 **Draw your face and write.**

Me!

blue
brown
green
big
small
short
long

I have _____ eyes.
I have a _____ mouth.
I have _____ hair.

Language: *have* for possession *I have (a small mouth).*

Starters Reading and Writing

1 Read and write.

A monster

I'm a happy monster. My _____head_____ is very big. I have long pink

(1) _____ . I have three (2) _____ . On my face,

my (3) _____ is small, but I don't have a small mouth.

In my mouth, I have big (4) _____ .

I have a pet. My pet is a (5) _____ .

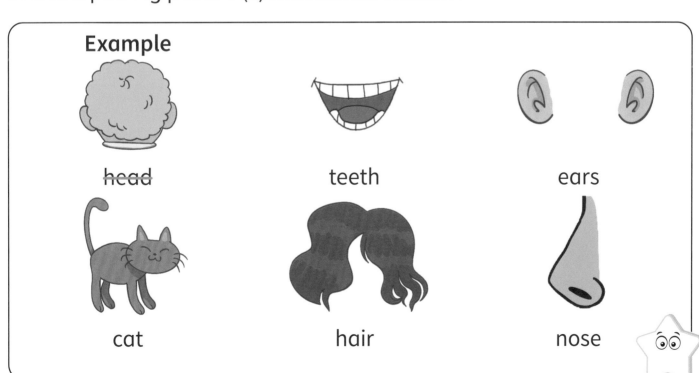

Example

| head | teeth | ears |
| cat | hair | nose |

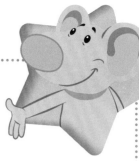

1 **Look and write.**

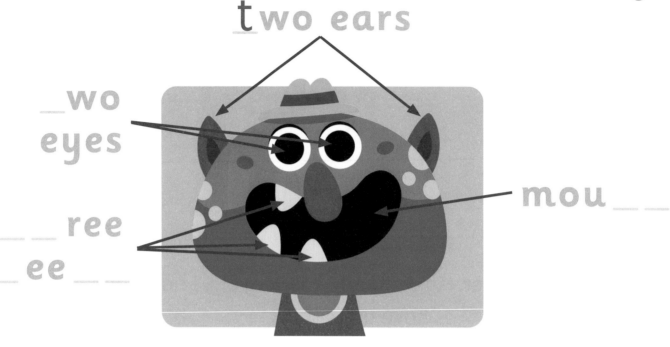

two ears

_wo
eyes

___ ree

__ ee __

mou ___

2 **Read and draw.**

I'm Mrs. Monster.
I have three teeth.

I'm Mr. Monster.
I have one tooth.

My picture dictionary

 1 **Find and stick.**

ears	eyes	mouth
nose	hair	teeth

My star card

 2 **Say the words. Color the stars.**

Marie's science

How do we use our senses?

1 🎧 24 **Listen and write the number. Look and circle.**

The rabbit has big ears / hands.

The fish has big ears / eyes.

His (nose) / hand is in the flowers. 1

The horse has big hands / teeth.

The girl feels the cat with her hand / eye.

2 **Follow and write the words. Say.**

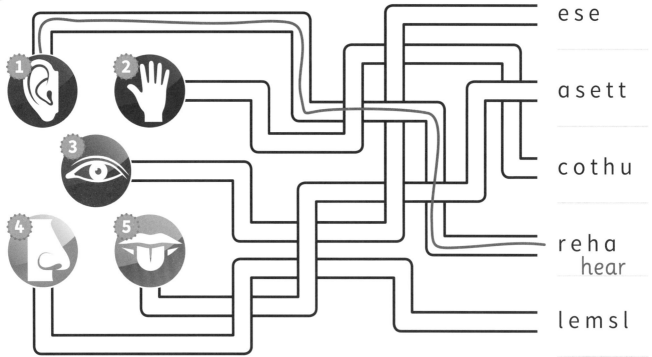

e s e

a s e t t

c o t h u

r e h a
hear

l e m s l

3 Now you! **Ask and answer.**

What can you hear?   I can hear birds.

Trevor's values

Take care of pets

Look, read, and match.

I brush my cat.

I wash my horse.

I feed my fish.

I walk my dog.

2 **Draw and write.**

Me!

This is my _____ . I _____ and _____ my _____ .

1 🎧 25 Listen and connect the dots.

2 Find and circle the words.

h	f	b	e	a	r	u	f	x
i	p	i	q	w	s	e	k	k
p	o	k	s	c	x	l	u	g
p	s	m	o	n	k	e	y	i
o	s	i	n	h	r	p	d	r
a	e	n	f	i	s	h	i	a
r	c	a	a	d	j	a	l	f
d	k	j	b	k	g	n	a	f
t	i	g	e	r	e	t	e	e

🖵 Do the online activities on **Practice Extra** as you complete this unit.

1 Read, look, and write "yes" or "no."

1 Are the giraffes sad?   no
2 Are the elephants happy?
3 Are the crocodiles long?
4 Are the snakes short?
5 Are the bears dirty?

2 Color the animals.

Now say. Color your friend's animals.

My giraffes are purple.

 26 **Listen and write the number. Color.**

2 **Look and put a ✓ or an X.**

Animals	hands	arms	legs	feet	tails
snakes	X	X	X	X	✓
bears					
birds					
monkeys					
crocodiles					
fish					
tigers					
giraffes					

Language: *have* for possession *They have (tails). They don't have (legs).*

Starters Reading and Writing

1 **Look and read. Write "yes" or "no."**

Example

The elephants have small ears.   no

Questions

1 The monkeys are on bikes.

2 The giraffes are under the elephants.

3 The tigers have red noses.

4 The crocodiles are next to the tigers.

5 The snakes have green eyes.

Monty's sounds and spelling

1 **Read, match, and say.**

Six king elephants.

Ten little hippos.

2 🎧 27 **Listen and write "a," "e," or "i."**

1. l e g

2. f __ sh

3. bl __ ck

4. b __ g

5. h __ ppo

6. p __ n

7. s __ ster

8. h __ nd

3 **Read and draw.**

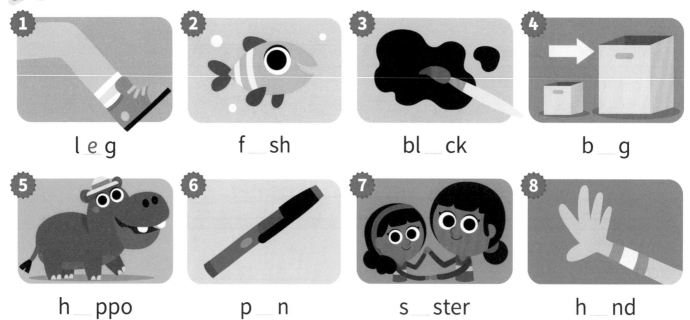

Little king elephant.

My picture dictionary

1 Find and stick.

crocodile	elephant	tiger
hippo	giraffe	snake

My star card

2 Say the words. Color the stars.

8 My clothes

1 Look, find, and circle the number. Say.

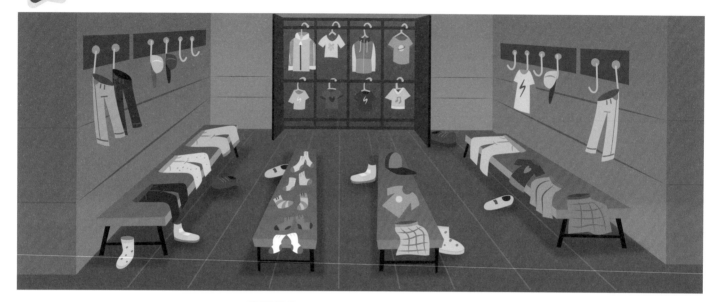

Seven pairs of pants.

pants	1	2	3	4	5	6	⑦	8	9	10
socks	1	2	3	4	5	6	7	8	9	10
T-shirts	1	2	3	4	5	6	7	8	9	10
skirts	1	2	3	4	5	6	7	8	9	10
shoes	1	2	3	4	5	6	7	8	9	10
jackets	1	2	3	4	5	6	7	8	9	10
caps	1	2	3	4	5	6	7	8	9	10

2  28 Listen and answer.   How many jackets?   Two!

Vocabulary: clothes   Do the online activities on **Practice Extra** as you complete this unit.

1  Listen and color.

2 Draw and write.

Me!

My favorite clothes are my _____ .

Sue

Nick

Kim

Tony

May

2 🎧 31 **Listen and match.**

Vocabulary: clothes | **Language:** *have* for possession *He/She has (a black shoe).*

Starters Listening

1 🎧 32 🐵 **Read the question. Listen and write a name or a number. There are two examples.**

3   ~~Kim~~   Tom   ~~10~~   8   Bill   9

Examples

What is the girl's name?   Kim

How old is she?   10

Questions

1 What is the dog's name?

2 How old is the dog?

3 What is the name of Kim's brother?

4 How old is Kim's brother?

5 How many children are in Kim's class?

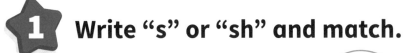
1 **Write "s" or "sh" and match.**

1 ___ kirt   **2** T-___ irt

3 ___ ocks   **4** ___ oes

2 **Read and draw.**

A crocodile in a red skirt and green socks.	A dog in purple shorts and orange shoes.

3 **Write the sentences.**

1

an orange   She has   skirt.

She has an orange skirt.

2

socks.   six blue   He has

3

They have   shorts.   white

My picture dictionary

 Find and stick.

jacket	shoes	skirt
socks	pants	T-shirt

My star card

 Say the words. Color the stars.

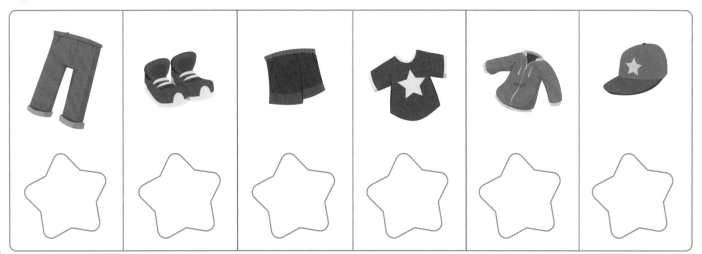

Marie's geography

Where do animals live?

1 Look and write "g" for garden, "p" for polar region, and "s" for savanna.

 g  p  s

     p

2 🎧 33 **Listen and circle.**

Habitat: forest / ⭕savanna⭕
Animals: lion / polar bear
Climate: hot / cold

Habitat: polar region / garden
Animals: penguin / tiger
Climate: hot / cold

Habitat: forest / garden
Animals: fox / zebra

3 Now you! **Write, draw, and say.**

In _____ (country) there is
a _____ (habitat) region. There are
_____ and _____ (animals).

Trevor's values

Love nature

 1 **Read and write the number.**

We can use less water. ☐ 3

Recycling is fun! ☐

We can plant a tree. ☐

We can keep parks clean. ☐

 2 **Draw and write.**

I love nature!

I _____ to help nature.

1 Read, draw, and color.

Ben

Bill

Bill
~~short shoes~~
a dirty T-shirt
a big nose
a sad mouth
a red jacket
long black hair

Ben
big shoes
a happy mouth
green hair
a small nose
purple pants
short red hair

 2 🎧 34 Listen and say "Bill" or "Ben."

3 Say the sentences.   Fish and snakes don't have legs.

 and  no legs.

 and 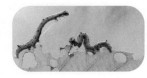 no hands.

 and  no arms.

 and  no hair.

4 Look, read, and write.

arms　　ears　　~~face~~　　hands　　mouth　　tail　　two　　two

At the safari park

I'm small and brown. I have a funny **(1)** _face_

2

with **(2)** _____ big **(3)** _____ and a big **(4)** _____ .

My **(5)** _____ are long, and

2

I have **(6)** _____

big **(7)** _____ . I have

a long **(8)** _____ .

9 Fun time!

1 35 Listen and write the number.

 1

2 Look and match.

1
2
3

swim

play the guitar

play tennis

ride a bike

play soccer

play basketball

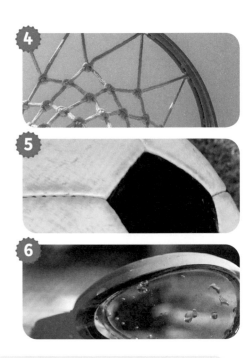

4
5
6

Vocabulary: sports and leisure   ⬚ Do the online activities on **Practice Extra** as you complete this unit.

1 Find and circle six words.

? a ?

w	a	s	g	r	i	d	e
r	s	p	u	g	i	t	a
a	w	b	i	k	e	r	p
t	i	n	t	i	s	l	l
o	m	l	a	s	t	c	a
o	m	e	r	x	u	r	y
t	e	n	n	i	s	a	e

? ?

?

play the ?

2 Look and write.

soccer ~~guitar~~ play ride swim tennis

1 play the ___guitar___
2 ___ basketball
3 play ___

4 play ___
5 ___ a bike
6 ___

1 🎧 36 **Listen and put a ✓ or an ✗.**

2 **What can you do? Draw and write.**

Me!

✓	✗
✓	✗

I can _____

I can't _____

_____ . _____ .

Language: *can* for ability *I/You can (play tennis). He/She can't (swim).*

Starters Reading and Writing

1 Look and write the words.

Example

b s k a t e

b l l a

b a s k e t b a l l

Questions

1 _____

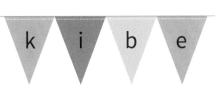

k i b e

2 _____

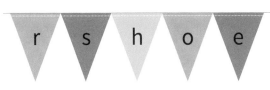

r s h o e

3 _____

n i n e t s

4 _____

t a g u i r

5 _____

o r e c s c

Monty's sounds and spelling

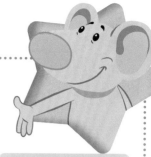

1 **Look and write. Complete the table.**

snail   day   play
train   ~~say~~   tail

ay	ai
say	tail

s a y

October
22

2 **Match to make sentences. Say and write.**

We can play tennis.

We can	play	a bike.
I can't	play	the piano.
We can't	play	tennis.
They can	ride	a game.

3 **Read, draw, and write the answer.**

What can you play on a gray day?

My picture dictionary

1 Find and stick.

play basketball	ride a bike	play tennis
swim	play soccer	play the guitar

My star card

2 Say the words. Color the stars.

10 At the amusement park

1 Look and write.

bike   boat   bus   car   ~~helicopter~~
truck   motorcycle   plane   train

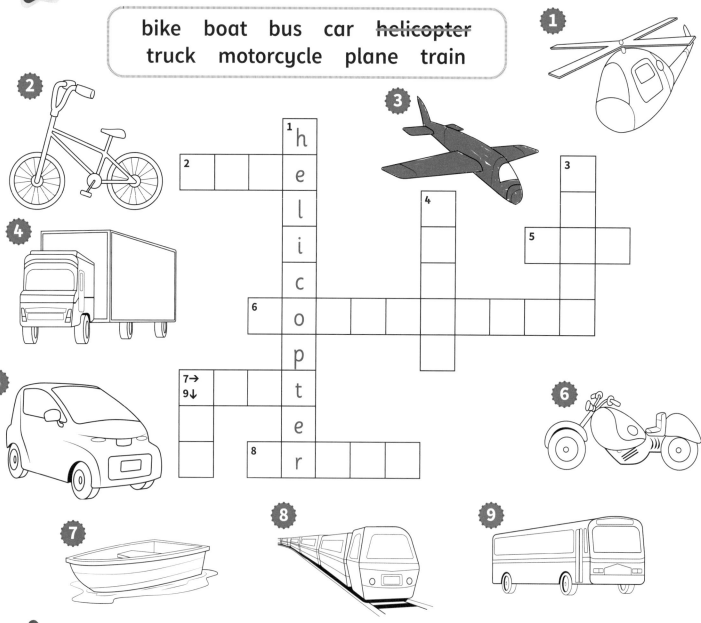

2 🎧 37 Listen and color.

Draw stars in, on, under, or next to the pictures.

☆

Now ask and answer. Draw your friend's stars.

Where's the star?   It's under the bus.

 Look and write.

> ~~truck~~   ~~T-shirt~~   helicopter   boat   pants   plane
> skirt   jacket   cap   motorcycle   shorts   bus

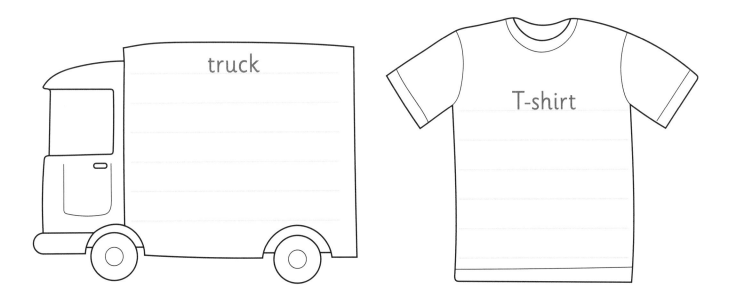

truck

T-shirt

1 🎧 38 **Listen and draw colored lines.**

 2 **Draw and write. Say.**

I'm riding a horse.

riding   horse   bike   motorcycle   driving
truck   bus   boat   flying   plane   helicopter

Me!

I'm _____ a _____ .

Language: present progressive for ongoing actions *What are you doing? (I'm riding a horse).*

Starters Listening

1 🎧 39 🐵 **Listen and check (✓) the box. There is one example.**

Where is the truck?

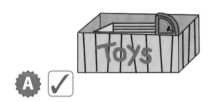 **A** ✓

 **B** ☐

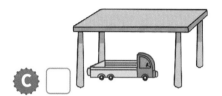 **C** ☐

1 What's Anna doing?

 **A** ☐

 **B** ☐

 **C** ☐

2 What toy is under the chair?

 **A** ☐

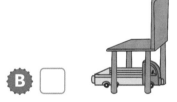 **B** ☐

 **C** ☐

3 What color is Matt's motorcycle?

 **A** ☐

 **B** ☐

 **C** ☐

4 Which boy is Alex?

 **A** ☐

 **B** ☐

 **C** ☐

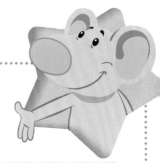

 1 **Read and circle "ng." Choose and draw.**

1 I'm flyi(ng) my plane.

2 I'm singing a song.

3 I'm riding my motorcycle.

4 I'm clapping my hands.

 2 **Look and write.**

clapping   ~~singing~~

flying

my hands   a helicopter

~~a song~~

1
I'm singing   a song.

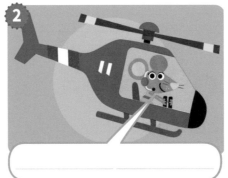
2

3

 3 **Read and write.**

flying   ~~driving~~   riding   flying   driving   riding

1 I'm _____driving_____ a truck.

2 I'm _____ a plane.

3 You're _____
a motorcycle.

4 You're _____ a car.

5 I'm _____ a horse.

6 You're _____
a helicopter.

My picture dictionary

 Find and stick.

bus	truck	motorcycle
helicopter	plane	ship

My star card

 Say the words. Color the stars.

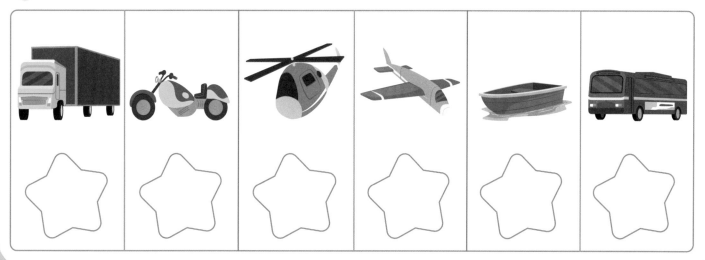

Marie's geography

How do we travel?

1 **Look and write the number.**

1 road 2 water 3 air 4 rail

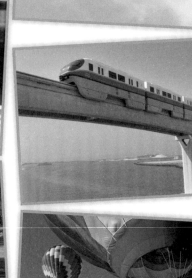

3

2 **Read and match. Draw lines.**

1 A helicopter travels …   … on the road.
2 A ship travels …   … on the water.
3 A train travels …   … on rails.
4 A scooter travels …   … in the air.

3 Now you! **Now you! Ask and answer.**

(It travels in the air.) (A helicopter?) (No!) (A plane?) (Yes!)

Geography: travel | critical thinking

Trevor's values

Work together

1 Read and write the number.

1

1 (Give me your hand. I can help you.)   3 (Here's some water.)

2 (Let's work together. We can do it.)   4 (We're a team – let's go!)

1 🎧 40 **Listen and draw lines. There is one example.**

Alex   Dan   Grace   Hugo

May   Bill   Sue

Follow the lines and write.

bedroom ~~living room~~ kitchen hallway

living room

 Draw your house. Write and say.

Me!

My house has

 **41** # Listen and color the stars.

2 Match and write.

1 She's drawing a _____picture_____ .

2 He's reading a _____ .

3 She's sitting on a _____ .

4 They're listening to _____ .

5 He's driving a _____ .

6 They're playing a _____ .

 chair

 video game

 car

 book

 music

 picture

Language: present progressive *What's he/she doing? He's/She's (driving a car).*

Starters Reading and Writing

1 Look, read, and write. Use one word.

Examples

Where are the children?   in the ___kitchen___

How many people are there?   ___two___

Questions

1 What's the girl eating?   some _____

2 What's does the boy have?   a _____

3 What's the girl doing?   listening to _____

4 What animals can the boy see?   _____

5 Who is pointing?   the _____

Monty's sounds and spelling

 1 **Read and write. Look and circle "yes" or "no."**

1 The monkey's watching TV in the bedroo___.  yes / **no**

2 The ___ouse's riding a bike in the dining roo___.  yes / no

3 Grand___a's singing in the hallway.  yes / no

4 A horse's cooking in the kitchen.  yes / no

 2 **Choose and write. Draw and write.**

> ~~monkey~~ mouse hippo singing
> ~~riding a motorcycle~~ playing the guitar
> bedroom living room ~~dining room~~

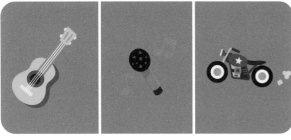

The monkey's riding a motorcycle in the dining room.

My picture dictionary

1 Find and stick.

? ? ? ? living room	? ? ? ? bedroom	? ? ? ? kitchen
? ? ? ? bathroom	? ? ? ? hallway	? ? ? ? dining room

 # My star card

2 Say the words. Color the stars.

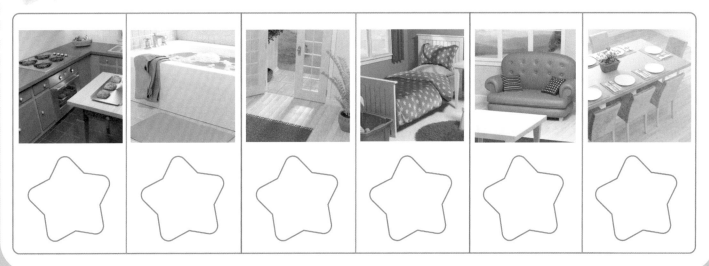

12 Party time!

1 🎧 42 **Listen and color.**

2 **Find, circle, and write.**

a	w	e	i	f	i	s	h	s
c	h	o	c	o	l	a	t	e
a	b	r	e	c	k	f	a	m
k	l	t	c	h	e	j	p	r
e	b	u	r	g	e	r	p	o
p	r	o	e	v	i	s	l	b
b	a	n	a	n	a	t	e	g
j	z	o	m	e	r	s	t	u
o	r	a	n	g	e	v	i	e

1   apple

5 ____

2 ____

6 ____

3 ____

7 ____

4 ____

8 ____

1 Look and write.

1 → cat

2 →

3 →

4 →

2 Read and write.

young
~~eating~~
banana
cake

The small monkey's ___eating___ an orange, and the big monkey has some _____. The old monkey's eating a _____, and the _____ monkey has some ice cream.

1 🎧 43 Listen and put a ✓ or an ✗.

1 ✓

2

3

4

2 Look and write "like" or "don't like."

Me!

I _____ fish.

Me!

I _____ burgers.

Me!

I _____ ice cream.

Me!

I _____ .

Language: present simple *I like (fish). I don't like (burgers).*

Starters Listening

1 🎧 44 🐵 **Listen and color. There is one example.**

monty's sounds and spelling

1 Look, write, and match.

1
2
3
4
5
6
7
8
9
10
11
12
13

tr a i n	5	___ock	☐
___ainbow	☐	___lephan___	☐
___oll	☐	___oe	☐
h___	☐	h___ppo	☐
___ouse	☐	si___	☐
___ook	☐	___encil	☐
tee___	☐		

2 Think and write. Then draw.

1 The _____ and the _____ are playing the piano.

2 My pet _____ likes to wear _____.

3 On the train there's a green _____, a purple _____,
and a beautiful _____.

3 Look and circle the words. Say.

mousehipporainbowpenbookridingredhappyteethtrain

My picture dictionary

1 Find and stick.

kiwi	apple	burger
cake	chocolate	ice cream

My star card

2 Say the words. Color the stars.

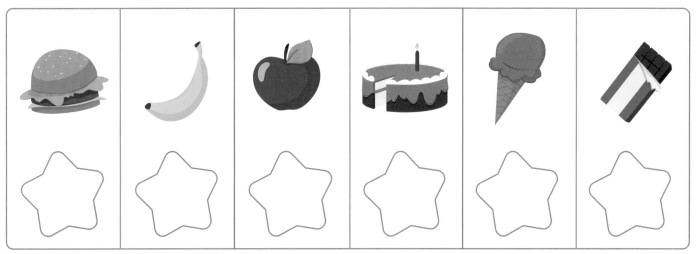

Marie's science

How does fruit grow?

 1 **Look and match. Say.**

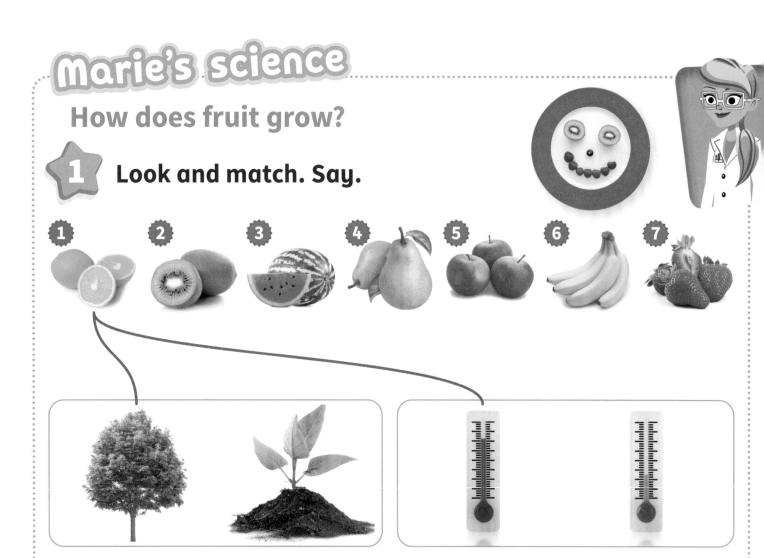

 2 **Read and write.**

> the ground   trees   big   ~~hot~~   small   strawberries

1 Oranges grow in _____ hot _____ places.
2 _____ grow on plants in cold places.
3 Watermelons are very _____ and grow on the ground.
4 Bananas grow on _____ in hot places.
5 An apple tree is big, but a strawberry plant is _____.
6 Some fruit grows on trees, and some grows near _____.

 3 Now you! **Ask and answer.**

Watermelons?   They grow on the ground in hot countries.

Trevor's values

Keep clean

 Number the pictures in order.

A

 2

 3

 1

B

C

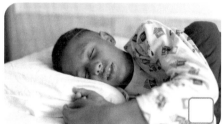

 Look, read, and write.

> teeth　apples　hands

He's washing his

She's brushing her

She's washing her

Review Units 9, 10, 11, and 12

1 Check (✓) one box for each monster.

reading a book						
eating fish						
watching TV						
taking a bath						

Now ask and answer. Check (✓) your friend's boxes.

What's the old monster doing?   He's eating fish.

reading a book						
eating fish						
watching TV						
taking a bath						

2 **Circle the different word. Say.**

1 kiwi   apple   orange   (guitar)
2 truck   ice cream   train   bus
3 burger   tiger   giraffe   lion
4 bathroom   kitchen   bedroom   chocolate
5 motorcycle   helicopter   hallway   truck
6 play   swim   plane   ride

 3 **Read and write. Draw.**

Me!

I'm _____ .

I'm at home in the kitchen. I like _____ , but I don't like _____ .

My favorite food is _____ .

Grammar reference

1 **Order the questions. Write the number.**

1 (your) ☐ (name?) ☐ (What's) ☐

2 (old) ☐ (are) ☐ (you?) ☐ (How) ☐

 2 **Read and circle.**

1 He's / She's Scott.   He's / She's six.

2 He's / She's Sally.   He's / She's seven.

3 **Read and write.**

| isn't   Is   Is   is |

1 _____ your ball in your car?   Yes, it _____ .

2 _____ your ball on the table?   No, it _____ .

4 **Circle the sentences.**

Wearen'tsad.We'rehappy.Arewebeautiful?

Read and write.

They're   It's

1 Look at the dog. _____ long.
2 Look at the two cats. _____ small.

 Order the words. Write the sentences.

1 (face.) (have) (I) (a clean) _____

2 (You) (short) (hair.) (have) _____

7 Circle the sentences.

Theyhavetails.Theydon'thavehair.Dotheyhavelegs?

 Read and write.

doesn't have   has

1 ✓ He _____ your red pants.
2 ✗ He _____ your blue hat.

9 **Order the words. Write the sentences.**

1 (can) (sing.) (He) _____

2 (swim.) (They) (can't) _____

3 (ride) (Can) (you) (a bike?) _____

 10 **Read and write.**

(am   Are   not   Are)

1 _____ you flying a plane?   Yes, I _____ .

2 _____ you playing the guitar?   No, I'm _____ .

 11 **Circle the sentences.**

What'shedoing?He'stakingabath.Ishereading?

 12 **Read and write.**

(don't like   like   don't like   like)

1 ☺ I _____ cake.

2 ☹ I _____ ice cream.

3 ☹ I _____ fish.

4 ☺ I _____ apples.

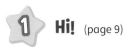

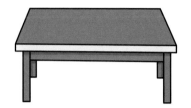

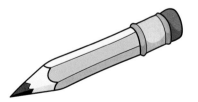

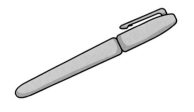

My family (page 29)

 Our pets (page 39)

 My face (page 45)

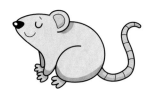

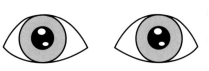

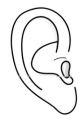 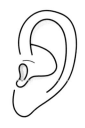

Wild animals (page 53)

 My clothes (page 59)

 Fun time! (page 69)

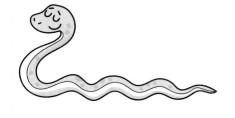

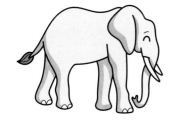

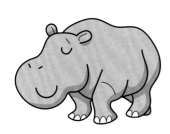

10 At the amusement park (page 75)

11 Our house (page 83)

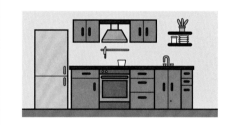

12 Party time! (page 89)